The Millennials' Guide

Navigating Workplace Communication

Table of Contents

Chapter 1. Introduction

Welcome to "The Millennials' Guide: Navigating Workplace Communication"! This Special Report is a vibrant, stimulating, and enriching toolkit, tailored specifically for millennials stepping into today's dynamic work environment. This isn't just another ordinary communication guide; it's a comprehensive blueprint brimming with meticulously curated insights, practical tips, real-world scenarios, and expert advice. Its pages hold the key to decoding the mystery of effective interactions, catering to your unique needs as a millennial. Ignite your career trajectory by mastering the art of impactful conversation with a sprinkle of millennial magic. With this Report in your arsenal, step into every office meeting or virtual team conference with a newfound confidence that speaks volumes about your potential. Take the reins of workplace communication. Let this Special Report be your compass in navigating the vast seas of professional interaction, empowering you to leave an indelible mark on your career. Purchase your copy today, kickstart your journey into the world of empowered communication, and start making a difference in your workplace and beyond!

Chapter 2. Understanding Generational Differences in Communication

To decode the puzzle of workplace communication, it's crucial to first comprehend the varying communication styles of different generations. This includes understanding the differences and similarities, appreciating the diversities, and learning to adapt. Armed with this knowledge, communication becomes smoother, relations become stronger, and collaborations become more fruitful.

2.1. The Generational Landscape

The landscape of recent workplaces is multi-generational. This includes individuals from the Silent Generation (born between 1928 and 1945), Baby Boomers (1946 - 1964), Generation X (1965 - 1980), Millennials, or Generation Y (1981 - 1996), and Generation Z (born after 1996). While it's important not to stereotype or box people, observing generational traits can provide useful insights into typical behaviors.

2.2. Defining Communication

At its core, communication involves exchanging information and ideas through multiple channels. This involves listening, speaking, observing, and empathizing. Each generation, based on its collective experiences, has a distinct preferred method of communication.

2.3. Silent Generation and Baby Boomers

The Silent Generation and the Baby Boomers, who have spearheaded some of the most significant advancements within workplaces, often prefer less digital communication. Face-to-face interaction, formal letters, telephone calls, and eventually, emails, have been their preferred communication methods.

These generations especially value respect, structure, and protocol in the workplace. They appreciate well-thought-out conversation and usually take time to draft detailed written responses. In terms of feedback, the preference generally is towards the discreet and individual rather than in groups or public forums.

2.4. Generation X

Generation X witnessed the advent of technology in communication. They are more comfortable with digital tools compared to their predecessors. Emails remain a strong preference for this generation, but they also adapt to newer forms like instant messaging or video conferencing.

This generation, often considered the 'middle child' in the workplace, balances traditional and modern communication approaches. They value clear guidelines but with the flexibility to implement them in required ways. They are known to prefer direct and immediate feedback.

2.5. Millennials or Generation Y

Millennials or Generation Y grew up with technology, causing a significant shift in communication trends. Text messages, social media and chat apps are second nature to them. Emails are used, but a quicker digital response is appreciated.

Millennials value transparency and accessibility. Open-dialogue and reciprocal feedback are key. Multi-tasking across different communication platforms comes easily to them. Video calls, collaboration tools, virtual conferences, are all part of their communication arsenal. They prefer flexible, inclusive yet digital environments.

2.6. Generation Z

Being digital natives, Generation Z tends to be fluent in a myriad of digital platforms for communication. Quick, visually appealing, and efficient methods like emojis, GIFs, and instant stories are popular. Collaboration happens not just through words, but visuals too.

Gen Z values authenticity, social connection, and immediate feedback. They tend to dislike lengthy, wordy communications, preferring bite-sized yet meaningful content. They are comfortable sharing their thoughts publicly and affirm their voice counts in the larger dialogue of workplace communication.

2.7. Bridging the Communication Gap

Bridging the communication gap between generations involves understanding, flexibility, and compromise. Here are some strategies:

- Encourage inter-generational mentoring: Pair younger employees with more experienced ones to share knowledge, insights, and communication nuances.

- Promote open dialogue: Discuss communication preferences openly. Share not only the 'how' but also 'why' behind those preferences.

- Provide training: Offer training on various communication tools to make all employees comfortable using different channels.

- Avoid jargon: Each generation has its lingo. Encourage use of clear, concise, and universally understood language.

- Respect all styles: Establish a culture that values all communication styles, fostering an environment of mutual respect.

- Foster an inclusive environment: Create spaces where all voices are heard. This boosts empathy levels, thus enhancing synergies and productivity.

2.8. In Conclusion

As workplaces evolve, so will the generational mix. It's important to value the richness of this diversity. Being cognizant of these differences, respectful of varying communication styles and adaptable, can offer multiple perspectives and solutions. This enhances collaboration, enriches workplace culture, and drives growth. So, while threading through the labyrinth of generational communication might seem taxing, the other side holds the treasure of a more inclusive, efficient, and thriving professional environment.

Chapter 3. Navigating Workplace Hierarchy: Bosses, Colleagues, and Subordinates

Navigating hierarchical relationships in the corporate world is a key skill to master for effective communication and career progression. Understanding the dynamics of each relationship category - your superiors, peers, and subordinates - is crucial.

3.1. Understanding Your Boss

Your relationship with your boss is central to your job satisfaction and career advancement opportunities. Recognizing their working style, communication preference, and expectations can put you in a favorable position.

Firstly, grasp the underlying aspects of their management style: Are they hands-on or hands-off? Do they prefer weekly updates or summaries at the end of the month? Are they purely work-focused or do they encourage a friendly work environment? Answering these questions will help you adapt your communication and working style to your boss's preferences, thereby fostering a healthy rapport.

Efficient communication with your boss revolves around clarity, conciseness, and ownership. Be transparent in your updates, concisely relaying the progress of your projects, nuances you encountered, and the solutions implemented.

3.2. Building Relationships with Colleagues

Peer relationships hold a unique place in the workplace hierarchy. These relationships can offer support, promote a healthy work environment, and create opportunities for collaboration.

Active listening plays a significant role when communicating with peers. Show empathy, be open to their ideas and make sure your responses are constructive and supportive. A collaborative mindset fosters an environment of mutual growth and productivity.

Networking is instrumental in building sound peer relationships. Use company events, training programs, or team activities as opportunities to connect with your colleagues. Establishing these connections can lead to cross-functional collaboration, further helping career development.

3.3. Leading and Communicating with Subordinates

If you're in a managerial position, your leadership skill and your ability to communicate effectively with your team can directly impact their performance.

Two-way communication is essential when dealing with subordinates; encourage them to share their ideas and feedback. This approach fosters a sense of involvement, leading to increased job satisfaction and productivity.

Acknowledge their accomplishments - this reassures them that their work is valued and appreciated. Provide constructive feedback when necessary; remember that the goal of feedback is to improve, not to criticize.

Regular team meetings are beneficial, as is setting clear, measurable expectations and ensuring each team member understands their roles and responsibilities. Check in regularly to offer guidance, assistance, and ensure that they're heading in the right direction.

3.4. Understanding the Power Dynamics

Every workplace has its politics and power dynamics – understanding these is integral to thriving professionally.

Stay keenly alert to the subtleties of interactions, whether it's during meetings, office chats, or emails. This will help you understand office dynamics and alliances, and navigate situations strategically.

Deal with office politics ethically. Avoid gossip and don't engage in backstabbing. Instead, focus on building positive relationships and managing conflicts professionally. Moreover, try to maintain a balanced perspective; don't let office politics demoralize or distract you from your work.

Understanding power dynamics also involves understanding the influencers in your organization. Recognizing the individuals who have informal yet significant clout can help in predicting decision-making patterns and strategically positioning your ideas.

3.5. Conclusion

Navigating your workplace hierarchy effectively can have significant benefits for your career growth and job satisfaction. Ultimately, the key to dealing with bosses, colleagues, and subordinates lies in understanding individual needs, effective communication, empathy, and constructive collaboration. Boost your career trajectory by mastering these aspects of workplace relationships. Remember, every interaction you have at work contributes to your professional growth and success.

Chapter 4. Mastering Digital Communication: Email, Slack, and Beyond

In this age of rapid digitization, mastering digital communication is no longer optional, but a necessity. The ability to communicate effectively on platforms such as Email, Slack, or other business communication software is a key factor that amplifies your professional brand image and productivity.

4.1. Understanding the Digital Communication Landscape

Digital communication encompasses a wide variety of platforms and methods. You might utilize emails, instant messaging apps, project management tools, social media, and video conferencing software – each with its own rules of engagement. Though the formats may vary, the purpose remains the same: to transmit information quickly, clearly, and effectively.

Today, companies often use a combination of different tools to ensure efficient and seamless communication. However, the two most predominately used platforms are email and instant communication apps like Slack, Teams, or WhatsApp. To communicate effectively, one must understand the proper usage and significance of each.

4.2. The Art of Professional Email Communication

Email is a formal and official form of communication. It allows for in-depth discussions, handles internal and external correspondences, and is used to document important information. Here are some practical tips on mastering email etiquette:

Be Professional: Keep your tone professional and respectful in your emails. Avoid using caps, as it suggests shouting.

Write a Concise Subject: Be precise and informative in your subject line. It sets the stage for the recipient, letting them know the general content of your email.

Keep it Simple and Clear: Write clear and short sentences. Use bullet points if needed, as lengthy paragraphs can be hard to read.

Include a Proper Salutation and Closing: Begin with a professional greeting and close with an appropriate sign-off.

Use the CC and BCC Fields Judiciously: Do not spam the inbox of the people not directly involved in the conversation.

Use attachments wisely: Compress files when possible and provide a brief description of the attachments in the body of the email for reference.

Proofread: Always proofread your emails for grammatical errors and clarity of message before sending.

Remember, it's always better to be too formal in an email than too casual, especially when dealing with clients or superiors.

4.3. Instant Messaging and How it Works

While email is more formal and can be used for longer, more intricate messages, apps like Slack, Teams, and WhatsApp are perfect for quick updates, reminders, or brief discussions. Here's how to harness the power of instant messaging apps proficiently:

Stay Professional: Although it's a less formal medium, remember to maintain workplace decorum. Avoid using slang, and remember to remain respectful at all times.

Respect Time Zones: If your workspace consists of a global team, be mindful of someone's work hours while sending them a message. You wouldn't want to disturb them after their office hours.

Use Personal Messages and Channels Wisely: Slack and similar platforms offer the ability to create separate channels for different discussions and private messaging for one-on-one conversations. Understand when to use which.

Mind the Notifications: If you're posting something that needs immediate recognition, consider tagging people. However, avoid over-tagging.

Know When to Take it Offline: Not everything can be efficiently discussed in a text. Know when a situation warrants a face-to-face (or Video) conversation.

4.4. Integrating Digital Platforms: Finding the Balance

Managing your professional communication across various platforms can be tricky. Yet, striking the right balance is crucial to ensuring efficient workplace communication. There are specific things to consider:

Emails vs. Instant Messaging: Understand the nuances of when to use emails and when to resort to instant messaging. Important, official, and formal communications are usually best done through email. For quick queries, tasks, and non-official discussions, instant messaging applications are the go-to.

The Relevance of Video Conferencing: In a world where remote work is becoming more common, video calls are a crucial aspect of digital communication. They provide the personal touch of face-to-face communication while maintaining the convenience of digital connectivity.

Using Project Management Tools: Tools like Asana, Trello, and JIRA are a great way to assign tasks, track progress, and ensure everyone's on the same page. They help to keep communication about a particular task or project focused and in one place.

The key to effective digital communication lies in understanding each platform's strengths, limitations, and best uses. When done right, digital communication can not only boost your efficiency but also enhance your professional image.

4.5. Conclusion: Embracing the Digital Transformation

Mastering the art of digital communication is an ongoing process that demands continuous learning and practice. By adapting to the growing dynamic needs and trends, millennials can become the game-changers that the professional field requires.

Remember, good digital communication is about more than just sending messages - it's about building relationships and fostering an environment of mutual respect and understanding. It's about making communication effective, timely, engaging, and beneficial for everyone involved.

Start today. Revolutionize your digital communication skills, outshine in your workplace, and step onto the next exciting chapter of your professional growth.

Chapter 5. The Art of Virtual Meeting Etiquette

In the world of professional communication, there's no denying the growing importance of virtual meetings. With remote work becoming increasingly popular, grasping the essence of virtual meeting etiquette can help give you the edge in terms of professionalism and productivity.

5.1. The Significance of Virtual Meeting Etiquette

Virtual meeting etiquette is more than an unwritten code of manners; it's a crucial component carved out by the needs of the digital world that impacts the efficiency of digital interactions. The professionalism and respect you display during virtual meetings often contribute to your credibility and influence at the workplace. Moreover, just like any social situation, well-observed etiquette contributes to the smooth flow of proceedings and eases any friction that may arise in technology-mediated meetings.

5.2. Essential Virtual Meeting Etiquettes

Let's dive into the main aspects of virtual meeting etiquette that every millennial should master.

Chapter 6. Be on time: Punctuality

Being punctual for a virtual meeting is as relevant as it is for an in-person appointment. Implementing this principle shows respect for the time of others involved, creating a positive impression. Remember to join the meeting a few minutes in advance to ensure your technology is working well.

Chapter 7. Dress professionally: Presentation

Work-from-home often predisposes us to dress casually. However, align your dressing as per your office culture even while working remotely. Professionalism, even in attire, affects how others perceive us and how seriously they take our input.

Chapter 8. Mute appropriately: Sound management

Keeping your mike on mute when not speaking is of utmost importance in a virtual meeting. It prevents noise interrupting the speaker, fostering a more focused environment.

Chapter 9. Do not multi-task: Active participation

Active participation is a critical aspect of successful communication in virtual meetings. Resist the temptation to multi-task, stay engaged, and handle each query or task with your undivided attention.

Chapter 10. Limit distractions: Environment

Keeping your surroundings distraction-free not only helps maintain your focus, but also shows respect to all the participants. Always ensure to mute any potentially disruptive background sounds.

10.1. The ABC's of Proper Virtual Meeting Set-up

How you set up for your virtual meetings is just as important as your behavior during the meeting. Here's how to nail it:

Chapter 11. Adequate technology:

Ensure a stable internet connection and a high-quality microphone and webcam. Test out your equipment before the meeting to help prevent or resolve any technical issues that may arise.

Chapter 12. Background:

An appropriate and clean background is fundamental. Clear all clutter from the meeting view to present a professional image and to avoid any potential distractions.

Chapter 13. Comfort:

Ensure you are sitting in a comfortable place to focus better and stay engaged during the meeting. Adjust your camera to show your face clearly.

13.1. Setting the Mood Right: Body Language and Tone

Virtual meetings might create a barrier when it comes to communication, but being conscious about your body language and tone can bridge that gap to a substantial extent.

Chapter 14. Body language:

Keep your body language relaxed yet confident. Maintain eye contact by periodically looking at your webcam.

Chapter 15. Tone:

Your vocal inflections can express your attentiveness and energy. Speak clearly, keep your volume consistent, and make sure your voice carries positive and constructive energy.

15.1. Bringing it all together: Running Virtual Meetings Effectively

As a professional, it's likely you'll either attend or run virtual meetings. Here are some considerations to keep these meetings effective:

Chapter 16. Setting the meeting agenda beforehand:

Sending out an agenda before the meeting helps attendees prepare. It ensures meetings stay on track, leading to more fruitful discussions.

Chapter 17. Keeping track of time:

Sticking to the scheduled start and end times proves your respect for attendees' time and keeps discussions focused.

Chapter 18. Engage everyone:

Set an inclusive environment where everyone's opinion is valued.

Chapter 19. Follow-up:

After the meeting, send a summary of the key points discussed or action items to keep everyone on the same page.

By mastering these strategies, you as a millennial, will be optimally prepared to handle any virtual communication scenario thrown your way. Remember that etiquette is often about making others feel comfortable and valued. Whether a technician, artist, or manager, strong virtual meeting etiquette is an invaluable resource in your professional toolkit. The art of professional communication is ever-evolving, and your willingness to adapt reflects on your character and work ethic.

Chapter 20. The Power of Effective Listening in the Workspace

Good listening skills are often overlooked when discussing professional competencies. Yet, they are the bedrock of effective communication and collaboration in the workplace. As a millennial navigating your professional journey, honing these skills can drastically amplify your career trajectory. Let's dive into the intricacies of effective listening.

20.1. The Basics: Defining Effective Listening

Effective listening goes beyond the act of merely hearing the sounds around you. It's an active process of understanding, comprehending, responding, and remembering what's communicated. To be an effective listener in the workplace, you must not only understand the message being conveyed, but also interpret the speaker's nuances, non-verbal cues, and intentions.

Active listening involves four distinct processes:

1. Receiving: This is the initial step involving the raw perception of the spoken message, including your awareness of the speaker's volume, pitch, rate, and inflection.

2. Understanding: This step involves decoding the speaker's message and making sense of it. Here, you consider the speaker's words, grammar, and language use.

3. Remembering: An essential component of effective listening, remembering entails retaining what you've heard for future

application.

4. Responding: Lastly, this involves giving feedback demonstrating your understanding of the speaker's message.

20.2. The Dynamics: Why Is Effective Listening Crucial?

In the work environment, effective listening is instrumental in bridging gaps, fostering better understanding, promoting open dialogue, and inflating productivity. It facilitates smooth collaboration, solves complex problems, and nurtures respect among team members.

Here are few reasons why effective listening is vital:

1. Builds Trust: Displays respect for the speaker and their ideas, creating a conducive environment for open, honest communication.

2. Fosters Team Harmony: Reduces misunderstandings and conflicts while promoting effective team cohesiveness.

3. Enhances Knowledge: Valuable insights and knowledge can be obtained listening to diverse ideas and viewpoints.

4. Augments Problem-Solving: By grasping the full context of an issue, adapted and effective solutions can be devised.

20.3. The Spectrum: Types of Listening

Understanding the different types of listening is the next step in mastering this skill.

1. Appreciative Listening: Involves enjoying the message being

communicated, like listening to an engaging presentation or motivating speech.

2. Informative Listening: Focuses on understanding and interpreting the speaker's message, used frequently in meetings and seminars.

3. Empathetic Listening: Involves understanding the speaker's feelings, emotions, and perspective; crucial during one-on-one meetings or when managing team conflicts.

4. Analytical Listening: Involves understanding and evaluating the speaker's message from different viewpoints. Used frequently in decision-making scenarios.

20.4. Tips to Enhance Your Listening Skills

Now you understand the concept and importance of effective listening, let's delve into some tips to develop this skill:

1. Maintain Eye Contact: This non-verbal cue signals to the speaker that they have your undivided attention.

2. Be Open-minded: Refrain from judging or disagreeing with the speaker in your mind while they're still talking.

3. Avoid Distractions: Put away any digital devices and refrain from multi-tasking.

4. Reflect and Paraphrase: By restating the speaker's message, you demonstrate your understanding and openness to clarification, if needed.

5. Ask Informed Questions: This shows your active engagement with the speaker's message and allows you to gain deeper insights.

20.5. Overcoming Listening Barriers

Despite your best intentions, certain barriers can impede effective listening.

1. Noise and Distraction: Physical disruption can hinder understanding.

2. Prejudice and Bias: These can skew your interpretation of the speaker's message.

3. Language and Accent: Different language use or accents can cause comprehension difficulties.

4. Lack of Focus: Woolgathering or multitasking can disrupt the listening process.

Identify these barriers and strategize specific solutions to address them to optimize your listening capability.

20.6. Effective Listening and Emerging Digital Landscape

The digital age has elevated the importance of effective listening with remote and virtual communication becoming the norm. Active listening in virtual meetings can be more demanding due to the absence of physical non-verbal cues. However, by focusing on the speaker, refraining from multi-tasking, and providing clear feedback, you can overcome the challenges posed by the digital landscape.

Developing your listening skills can significantly complement your communication portfolio, strengthening your role within the workplace. As millennials, leveraging the power of effective listening allows you to foster better relationships, navigate complex multigenerational dynamics, and align your innovative ideas with team objectives. Strive to be the listener every speaker wants in their audience, and set the stage for your career growth by tapping into the power of effective listening.

Chapter 21. Building Resilient Work Relationships

A thriving professional life revolves not only around competent expertise in your respective field but also effective management of work relationships. Over the years, research has consistently highlighted the crucial role of robust relationships in workplaces. They catalyze productivity, foster an environment of collaborative work ethics, and contribute significantly towards creating harmonious office ecosystems. Building these relationships, especially in the fast-paced realm of a millennial's work life, is a skill that warrants dedicated attention. Employing resilience, understanding, empathy, and clarity in communication are a few key aspects that can cultivate strong and resilient work relationships.

21.1. Understanding Resilience in Work Relationships

Resilience is often considered the ability to bounce back in the face of adversity, but in the context of work relationships, it extends to being adaptable and open to change. It is forging relationships that withstand disagreements, conflicts, and varying perspectives. A resilient relationship is not about evading conflict, but about navigating through it with a problem-solving attitude, empathy, and open communication.

A resilient work relationship is a two-way street demanding consistent effort. Remember, the balance of power should be equal, and the respect should be mutual. Clear communication, active listening, empathy, and assertiveness fortify these resilient bonds.

21.2. The Foundation - Building Trust

Trust is the bedrock of any resilient relationship. Building trust and mutual dependability among coworkers isn't an overnight task; it's a steady process. Honesty, consistent behaviour, and reliability contribute towards cultivating an environment of trust. Employees who trust each other tend to work better collaboratively, are more open to giving and receiving feedback, and are less apprehensive about sharing ideas or concerns.

To manifest trust in your workplace relationships, follow through on your commitments, understand and respect the boundaries and competencies of others, convey your expectations clearly, and always communicate openly. Remember, nurturing trust is a continuous process.

21.3. Enhancing Communication

Communication is the lifeblood of resilient work relationships, with its importance surmounting beyond mere exchange of words. It encompasses active listening, understanding non-verbal cues, knowing when to speak, and mastering the art of conveying your point effectively and respectfully.

Good communication also involves appreciating diversity in thoughts and making an effort to understand ideas from different perspectives without prejudice. Employing empathy in your interactions can pave the way for meaningful and enriching communication.

21.4. Healthy Conflict Resolution

Conflicts are inevitable in any environment that encourages diversity of thought and is a testament to the healthy exchange of ideas.

Resilient relationships don't suppress conflicts but handle them effectively. Assertive communication where everyone's point of view is heard, understanding the root causes of the dispute, and arriving at a mutually beneficial solution are the pillars of healthy conflict resolution.

Also, acknowledging and apologizing for your mistakes, taking responsibility for your actions, and paving the way for constructive criticism are crucial aspects nurtured in a resilient work relationship.

21.5. Practicing Emotional Intelligence

Emotional Intelligence is understanding, using, and managing your own emotions positively to communicate effectively, empathize with others, overcome challenges, and defuse conflict. It plays a stellar role in building resilient work relationships. Being aware of your feelings, understanding others' emotions, and foregrounding this cognition to navigate through your relationships is the essence of emotional intelligence.

21.6. Cultivating Inclusivity and Respect for Diversity

In today's globalized world, workplaces often resemble melting pots of diverse individuals. Therefore, being open to diversity and promoting inclusivity can substantially boost the resilience of work relationships. Respecting and accepting a coworker's unique experiences, perspectives, and skills will create a more harmonious and productive work environment.

Recognizing and appreciating the diversity in your workplace and fostering an inclusive space can forge resilient work relationships, where everyone feels valued. This also cultivates a broader perspective and innovative ideas, further contributing to organizational success.

21.7. Coping with Professional Failures

In the journey of building robust professional relationships, setbacks could be encountered - be it project failures, missed opportunities, or conflicted interactions. Understanding that setbacks are part of the learning curve, and not a cumulative value of your abilities, is vital.

It's crucial to cling onto the resilient trait of bouncing back from these professional failures by introspecting, learning, and implementing lessons drawn from these experiences. Communicate clearly about your perceptions of the failure, learn from the feedback provided, and apply these learnings in the future endeavours.

21.8. Celebrating Success Together

One of the defining moments in cementing resilient work relationships is the collective joy of success. Reaching milestones or overcoming hurdles in a project calls for celebration as a team. Recognizing team members' contributions and appreciating the efforts fosters a sense of value and camaraderie, adding another layer to the resilience of relationships.

To sum up, building resilient work relationships requires understanding, patience, and a conscientious effort. It is the collective contribution of each individual in open conversations, maintaining trust, practicing emotional intelligence, resolving conflicts healthily, and valuing diversity. By shifting the focus on these aspects, a millennial can transform their work relationships and promote a welcoming, inclusive, and harmonious work environment.

Chapter 22. Workplace Conflict Management for Millennials

As millennials, conflict management in the workplace can often feel like navigating a minefield. It's challenging, and yet, it's an undeniable part of everyday work life, armed with what might initially seem like riddles wrapped in enigma. In this section, we'll dissect this intricate web, explore conflict resolution strategies, understand the role of communication, and learn how you, as a millennial, can effectively and confidently manage conflicts, in person or virtually.

22.1. Understanding Conflicts

Workplace conflicts usually arise from miscommunication, misunderstandings, or disagreements over roles, resources, or strategies. As millennials, your perspective might be quite different from your older colleagues' view, igniting potential tensions. However, conflicts aren't necessarily detrimental. If approached correctly, they can offer opportunities for growth, strengthening relationships, and better problem-solving. Therefore, understanding conflicts lays the foundation for effective conflict management.

For instance, consider a scenario where your team is faced with a disagreement about prioritizing projects. You're of the opinion that your client's website redesign should take precedence, whereas an older colleague insists that the e-commerce integration should be the priority. This forms a classic instance of workplace conflict.

22.2. The Role of Communication

Strong communication forms the heart of conflict resolution. It's critical to actively listen, articulate your thoughts clearly, and use the right tone and words. As millennials, adopting a communication style that balances assertiveness with respect can make a significant difference.

Imagine the same scenario as before. Instead of passionately arguing for your opinion, approach the situation respectfully by acknowledging your colleague's point of view, and then make your case. Emphasize upon well-articulated explanations. Supplementation of data or testimonials can also provide much-needed impetus. Here, communication holds the power to dissolve obstructions, making way for clarity and mutual consensus.

22.3. Conflict Resolution Strategies

Every conflict calls for a distinct strategy, and the right approach can prevent it from escalating into a full-blown crisis.

1. **Competing**: In scenarios where you need to enforce rules or defend your rights, assuming a competitive approach is advantageous. However, it should be implemented with care to avoid seeming aggressive.

2. **Collaborating**: When an innovative solution is required, and both parties' interests are significant, collaboration is a fruitful approach. As millennials, your knack for collaboration can truly shine in these situations.

3. **Compromise**: In instances where a quick or temporary solution is needed, or both parties have equal power, a compromise is advisable.

4. **Avoidance**: Sometimes, ignoring minor conflicts to focus on larger issues is the best course of action, especially when the

potential fallout outweighs the benefits.

5. **Accommodation**: If achieving harmony is more critical than winning an argument, accommodating the other party's needs can be a great strategy.

Remember, the priority isn't about winning, but about finding a resolution that supports collaboration, respect, and workplace harmony. Your millennial strength—capacity for empathy—can be an asset here.

22.4. Leveraging Emotional Intelligence (EQ)

As millennials, leveraging your emotional intelligence can aid in understanding others' perspectives, managing your emotions, and addressing conflicts effectively. EQ brings about better self-awareness, heightened understanding of others' emotions, and stronger interpersonal relationships—attributes that fuel successful conflict resolution.

For instance, if you notice your coworker is upset with you, instead of reacting defensively, use empathy to understand their view. Reflect on your actions and address the issue in a manner that assuages their grievances and strengthens your professional relationship.

22.5. Using Technology Effectively

In a world that's increasingly going digital, leveraging technology for conflict resolution is a different ballgame altogether. As digital natives, millennials are at an advantage. Virtual conflict resolution should involve:

1. **Active Listening**: Listen carefully to the other party's concerns, seeking clarification if needed.

2. **Non-verbal Cues**: Pay attention to facial expressions, tone of voice, and other non-verbal cues.

3. **Timely Communication**: Timely written communication can prevent misunderstandings.

4. **Professionalism**: Maintain professionalism in any digital communication.

Navigating conflict management as a millennial might seem daunting at first glance, but it's a significant aspect of your professional growth. By understanding conflicts, leveraging effective communication, choosing appropriate resolution strategies, and harnessing your emotional intelligence and digital skills, you can turn conflicts into opportunities. As a millennial, use your unique strengths and perspective to make conflict management a breeze and be a beacon of effective communication in the digital workplace landscape.

Chapter 23. Pitching and Presentation Skills for the Modern Work Environment

Excelling in workplace communication involves more than just efficient verbal and written skills. It necessitates mastering the art of crafting and delivering compelling pitches and engaging presentations.

23.1. Understanding Modern Work Environment

In today's digital age, where organizations are globally connected, and teams are often remote, presenting ideas or securing approval for projects can be a challenging task. The modern work milieu demands agility in communication techniques to bridge this virtual gap effectively. As a millennial, your goal should be to rise above this challenge and captivate your audience, whether it's through a physical conference room or via a virtual meeting platform.

For truly successful pitching and presentation, one must understand the intricacies of the modern work environment. This includes recognizing the need for concise, clear communication, knowing how to utilize technology effectively, understanding diversity, respecting time zones for international colleagues, and adapting to quick, dynamic changes.

23.2. The Art of Crafting a Pitch

Let's start by defining a pitch. A pitch is a precise, engaging summary of an idea or a product offered to a client or an investor. A successful pitch is designed to convince the listener to invest time, resources, or capital in your project.

Creating an effective pitch requires a keen understanding of your audience, your objective, and how your idea fits into the larger picture of what your team, department, or organization is trying to achieve. Here are the main steps to create a compelling pitch:

- Understand your audience: Recognize their needs, motivations, and values. The better you know your audience, the more specifically you can target your pitch to resonate with them.

- Define your message: Identify the core message of your pitch. Ensure it's clear, concise, and provides the necessary information.

- Tell a story: Engage your audience emotionally through a story that encapsulates your idea or project. Show them why your proposal is important, explain what problem it solves, or how it improves the situation.

- Practice, practice, and practice: The more you review and rehearse your pitch, the more polished it will sound, and the more confident you will feel.

23.3. Utilizing Technology in Presentations

Expertise in digital technology is a significant advantage that millennials possess over other generations. This skill can be crucial, especially when delivering presentations in a modern, virtually connected work environment.

From sharing screen content through collaborative platforms like Zoom, to making use of pulse surveys on tools like Slido during your presentation, technology can help you engage with your audience more effectively. Here are ways to use technology to your advantage:

- Visual Aids: Create interactive, visually appealing presentations using tools like PowerPoint or Prezi

- Polling or surveys: Engage the audience by using real-time polling during your presentations.

- Videos: Entrance your viewers by incorporating short, relevant videos into your presentation.

- Interactive tools: Use whiteboard features in platforms like Zoom or Microsoft Teams to highlight key points instantly.

23.4. Adapting Your Style for Virtual Presentations

Transitioning from face-to-face presentations to the virtual platform requires nuanced adaptation. Things like technical glitches, maintaining eye contact, body language, managing unreliable internet connections, ensuring sound clarity, and keeping your audience engaged across computer screens are new challenges that millennials should gear up to tackle.

Here are a few pointers:

- Check the technology beforehand: Ensure your microphone, video, and internet connection are functioning correctly.

- Maintain virtual eye contact: Look at the camera and not at the screen to give the impression of eye contact.

- Be mindful of body language: Use hand gestures naturally and make sure to maintain a good posture.

- Engage your audience: Involve your audience by asking questions, using the chat features, or running quick online polls.

23.5. Embracing Diversity and Inclusion

In the modern-day work world which is a melting pot of diverse cultures, races, and genders, one-size-fits-all communication no longer works. Millennials need to acknowledge and embrace this diversity in the workplace and incorporate this understanding into their pitching and presentation skills.

Understanding nuances of different cultures, celebrating different ideas and perspectives, respecting religious and statutory holidays, considering time zone differences, and using inclusive language are essential steps in developing presentations that resonate with everyone in your diverse team.

23.6. Handling Questions and Feedback

At the end of your pitch or presentation, be ready for questions or feedback. Show gratitude for inputs, answer questions confidently, and be open to critiques. Remember, every question or critique is an avenue for improvement and a chance to showcase your understanding and depth on the subject.

To summarize, effective presentation and pitching skills, teamed with the ability to adapt swiftly to the dynamic virtual environment of modern workplaces, can be a game-changing tool in your arsenal. With consistent practice, you can master these techniques and significantly enhance your communication effectiveness, leaving a lasting impression on your peers and superiors alike.

Chapter 24. Unlocking Your Emotional Intelligence for Better Communication

If you've entered a workplace having a misconception that logical, analytical, and technical skills are all you need to drive your career forward, you're in for a big surprise. In tandem with these skills, a stellar player in achieving success is Emotional Intelligence. A profound understanding and management of your emotions and those of people around you is integral to effective professional communication.

24.1. The Quintessence of Emotional Intelligence

Emotional Intelligence (EI), popularized by psychologist Daniel Goleman, refers to our ability to understand, use, and manage our emotions in positive ways to relieve stress, communicate effectively, empathize with others, overcome challenges, and defuse conflict. Indeed, the crux of good communication is often deeply rooted within the folds of EI.

You may ask, how does this connect to workplace communication? The answer is quite simple yet powerful. A sound EI helps you navigate conversations bearing a potentially negative or positive impact, thus minimizing misunderstanding and maximizing collaboration.

=== Recognizing the Components of Emotional Intelligence

Emotional Intelligence isn't a single skill but a composite of several soft skills delivered cohesively. Let's delve into these components:

1. Self-awareness: This entails recognizing your emotions and the effects they can have on your thoughts and actions. Recognizing your strengths and weaknesses, understanding what the triggers are, and knowing your values dictates this factor.

2. Self-regulation: We often face situations that test our patience and composure. The ability to efficiently control or redirect disruptive emotions and impulses, maintaining a balance, is what this quality depicts.

3. Motivation: A robust EI sees beyond money or status. It thrives on a passion for work that goes beyond career progression and is based on a deep affinity for the work itself and the perpetual desire to improve.

4. Empathy: Understanding the emotional state of your team members, responding to their feelings, validating their experiences, and fostering an environment of mutual respect and understanding makes you an empathetic communicator.

5. Social Skills: This last key element refers to handling social interactions, building networks, finding common ground with your peers, and maneuvering in the intricate web of workplace dynamics.

24.2. Unraveling the Interplay of Emotional Intelligence in Communication

Now that you have a good idea of the integral components of EI, let's explore how this melds with the broader scene of workplace communication.

In essence, EI works in the background of every conversation you have, dictate your tone, helps frame your words, and shapes the delivery of your message. Imagine conversing with a coworker; your emotional intelligence will govern how you decode their non-verbal cues, read between the lines, perceive their feelings, and respond appropriately.

Moreover, an emotionally intelligent individual will know when to step back and cool down when in heated situations, or when to stand up and speak out about an issue that's important.

=== Cultivating Emotional Intelligence: Practical Guidelines

Now, let's cut to the chase – how can you cultivate and fine-tune your emotional intelligence to enhance your communication? Here are some specific strategies:

1. Practice active listening: To truly understand what someone is trying to convey, it's important to actively listen. This means putting your own narrative or retort to pause and absorb what the other person has to say. Practice this by maintaining eye contact, nodding where appropriate, and summarizing their key points once they finished talking.

2. Start journaling: It's a simple, yet powerful, method of increasing self-awareness. You should write about your day, how you felt during different situations, how you reacted, and how you could have reacted better. This reflection can greatly improve your self-awareness and help you control your reactions better.

3. Exercise empathy: Always try and put yourself in the other person's shoes. This will give you a new perspective and make you a more open, understanding, and competent communicator.

24.3. Balancing Emotional Intelligence in the Virtual World

In the digital age, where emails and video conferences are prominent, your EI needs to evolve to fit these formats. For emails, it's important to consider things such as tone, politeness, clarity, and the potential impact of your words — something as simple as forgetting to say "thank you" can change the emotional hue of your message.

In virtual meetings, whilst face-to-face interaction might not be possible in this new reality, it's ever more critical to be sensitive to others' potential distractions or stresses. Remember the components of EI, stepping up to ease the tension and set an empathetic tone.

24.4. Conclusion: Emotional Intelligence as your Secret Weapon

In summary, Emotional Intelligence is an undervalued but absolutely crucial piece of the communication puzzle. Cultivating your EI will not only make you a more competent, understanding, and respectful individual, but it will also facilitate trustful relationships, foster collaborations, and create a more inclusive and harmonious work environment. Never underestimate the power of emotions in the workplace. Harness the strength of Emotional Intelligence, turn it into your secret weapon, and watch as your communication skills and, subsequently, your career, flourish.

With a polished EI, you can undoubtedly communicate more effectively, understand better, be understood better, and leave an impact that will put you on the fast track to a successful career in whatever field you chose.

Chapter 25. Shaping Leadership Communication Skills: Millennials in Command

The modern workplace represents an intricate web of communication. As a millennial, you're not only a part of this web but also a potential frontrunner in shaping its growth. Building your leadership skills depends heavily on your ability to communicate effectively. Let's embark on a journey to hone and refine these skills.

25.1. The Cornerstones of Leadership Communication

The bedrock of a powerful leadership lies in four primary dimensions: Clarity, Credibility, Connection, and Compassion. The essence of leadership communication can be distilled into these four Cs.

Clarity is the ability to express ideas and directions in a way that's easily understood by your team. Ensuring your message is clear entails eliminating unnecessary jargon, focusing on the core message, and reinforcing important points through repetition.

Credibility is, quite literally, believability. Your team trusts you when your actions align with your words. Be consistent, maintain transparency, and always follow through on your promises.

Connection means establishing and nurturing relationships with individuals in your team. When people feel connected to their leader, they're more motivated, engaged, and productive.

Compassion involves understanding and acknowledging your team's experiences, concerns, and aspirations. By being empathetic and supportive, you cultivate a positive and welcoming work environment.

25.2. Channel Your Inner Listener

Active listening is an essential yet underutilized communication skill. A great leader is also a great listener. Understand that listening goes beyond just hearing. It involves comprehending, interpreting, and responding in a way that adds value to the conversation. As a millennial leader, go beyond the text message; listen to ideas, apprehensions, tales of triumph, and even whispers of dissent that your team might communicate. Breathing life into your leadership communication means giving importance to every message, every story, and every voice.

25.3. The Millennial Magic: Harnessing Digital Communication

Navigating digital communication is second nature to millennials, and wielding this digital literacy in a leadership role will pay dividends. Email, virtual meetings, instant messaging, and project management software - all these tools offer a different lens through which to frame your communication.

Emails, while traditional, allow for detailed and thoughtful responses. Conversely, instant messaging caters to the fast-paced, hyperconnected millennial work environment. Yet, knowing when to use each medium can shape the style, resonance, and effectiveness of communication and consequent leadership.

25.4. The Juggling Act: Balancing Formal and Informal

The hierarchical nature of older workplaces is becoming increasingly obsolete, replaced with a more egalitarian structure. A millennial leader must balance the tightrope between formal and informal communication. Respectfully address disagreements, professionally manage conflicts, and unapologetically celebrate victories.

Never mistake casual language for casual commitment - even the most informal communication can convey the utmost professionalism.

25.5. Feedback: The North Star of Improvement

Feedback is crucial for growth. Encourage and practice open and constructive feedback. This two-way communication channel goes a long way in creating a supportive work environment wherein individuals understand their strengths and areas of improvement.

Giving feedback involves being specific, honest, and constructive. Receiving feedback, on the other hand, requires an open mind and the willingness to learn and grow.

25.6. Emotional Intelligence: The Unsung Hero

Emotional intelligence is the ability to recognize, understand, and manage our own emotions and the emotions of others. Leaders with high emotional intelligence can diffuse conflict, build stronger teams, and easily navigate changes.

Cultivating emotional intelligence translates to being self-aware, emotionally and socially competent. It includes regulating your emotions, showing empathy towards others, and nurturing relationships.

Your voyage towards shaping leadership communication skills begins with understanding your unique strengths, leveraging your digital savvy, and recognizing the importance of balance in professional communications. As millennial leaders arise, traditional boundaries are pushed aside, and exciting new landscapes appear on the horizon. Walk bravely, leading with empathy, clarity, and connection, and your steps will assuredly resound through the walkways of effective leadership communication. Let this journey redefine the command-scape of tomorrow.